Blastoff! Beginners are developed by literacy experts and educators to meet the needs of early readers. These engaging informational texts support young children as they begin reading about their world. Through simple language and high frequency words paired with crisp, colorful photos, Blastoff! Beginners launch young readers into the universe of independent reading.

Sight Words in This Book

and	go	people	to
at	have	play	up
blue	is	red	we
day	it	the	white
eat	of	they	

This edition first published in 2023 by Bellwether Media, Inc.

No part of this publication may be reproduced in whole or in part without written permission of the publisher. For information regarding permission, write to Bellwether Media, Inc., Attention: Permissions Department, 6012 Blue Circle Drive, Minnetonka, MN 55343.

Library of Congress Cataloging-in-Publication Data

Names: Sabelko, Rebecca, author.
Title: Independence Day / by Rebecca Sabelko.
Description: Minneapolis, MN : Bellwether Media, Inc., 2023. | Series: Blastoff! Beginners: Happy holidays! | Includes bibliographical references and index. | Audience: Ages 4-7 years | Audience: Grades K-1
Identifiers: LCCN 2022036397 (print) | LCCN 2022036398 (ebook) | ISBN 9798886871012 (Library Binding) | ISBN 9798886871890 (Paperback) | ISBN 9798886872279 (eBook)
Subjects: LCSH: Fourth of July--Juvenile literature.
Classification: LCC E286 .S123 2023 (print) | LCC E286 (ebook) | DDC 394.2634--dc23/eng/20220811
LC record available at https://lccn.loc.gov/2022036397
LC ebook record available at https://lccn.loc.gov/2022036398

Text copyright © 2023 by Bellwether Media, Inc. BLASTOFF! BEGINNERS and associated logos are trademarks and/or registered trademarks of Bellwether Media, Inc.

Editor: Christina Leaf   Designer: Laura Sowers

Printed in the United States of America, North Mankato, MN.

Table of Contents

It Is Independence Day!	4
A Day to Be Free	6
A Day of Summer Fun!	12
Independence Day Facts	22
Glossary	23
To Learn More	24
Index	24

It Is Independence Day!

Fireworks light up the sky. It is Independence Day!

fireworks

A Day to Be Free

Independence Day is July 4. We call it the Fourth of July.

The United States became free! It left **Great Britain.**

flag of Great Britain

People honor the U.S. They honor being free!

A Day of Summer Fun!

Families have **picnics**. They eat hamburgers. They eat hot dogs.

hot dog

hamburger

picnic

People play games outside. They go to the beach.

Cities have **parades**.
Bands play music.

parade

People wear red, white, and blue. They fly the flag.

People watch fireworks at night. Happy Fourth of July!

Independence Day Facts

Celebrating Independence Day

Independence Day Activities

have a picnic

go to the beach

fly the flag

Glossary

fireworks

colorful blasts of light in the sky

Great Britain

an old country in Europe that is now part of the United Kingdom

parades

people or groups who walk together during events

picnics

outside parties with food

To Learn More

ON THE WEB

FACTSURFER

Factsurfer.com gives you a safe, fun way to find more information.

1. Go to www.factsurfer.com.

2. Enter "Independence Day" into the search box and click .

3. Select your book cover to see a list of related content.

Index

bands, 16
beach, 14
cities, 16
families, 12
fireworks, 4, 5, 20
flag, 8, 18
free, 8, 10

games, 14
Great Britain, 8
hamburgers, 12
hot dogs, 12
July, 6, 20
music, 16

night, 20
parades, 16, 17
picnics, 12, 13
play, 14, 16
United States, 8, 10

The images in this book are reproduced through the courtesy of: Steve Cukrov, cover; chomplearn, p. 3; FamVeld, pp. 4-5; rblfmr, pp. 6-7; Stephen Rees, p. 8 (Great Britain); Nadia Leskovskaya, pp. 8-9; JasonDoiy, pp. 10-11; Excalibur_Media, p. 12 (hot dog, hamburger); kali9, pp. 12-13; Joe Sohm, pp. 14-15; Roberto Galan, p. 16; Frances L Fruit, pp. 16-17; SirinartCJ, p. 18; Wavebreakmedia, pp. 18-19, 22 (have a picnic); Design Pics Inc/ Alamy, pp. 20-21; NSphotostudio, p. 22 (celebrating); LeManna, p. 22 (go to the beach); Monkey Business Images, p. 22 (fly the flag); leventina, p. 23 (Great Britain); Sheila Fitzgerald, p. 23 (parades); M_a_y_a, p. 23 (picnics).